Understanding and Controlling Anger Workbook

A FAITH BASED APPROACH TO ANGER MANAGEMENT

Skip Pilgrim, Ph.D.

www.stressinterventionservices.com

Wendell "Skip" Pilgrim, Ph.D./Stress Intervention Services LLC
www.stressinterventionservices.com

Publisher's Note: This is a work of non-fiction. Book Layout © 2016 BookDesignTemplates.com

Understanding and Controlling Anger Workbook/ Wendell "Skip" Pilgrim, Ph.D. -- 1st ed.

Know this, my beloved brothers: let every person be quick to hear, slow to speak, slow to anger;

for the anger of man does not produce the righteousness of God. (James 1:19-20 ESV)

CONTENTS

Lesson 1 - Am I An Angry Person?

For I know my transgressions, and my sin is ever before me. (Psalms 51:3)

Anger Assessment Test:

1. I've had trouble on the job because of my temper. True or False

2. People say that I fly off the handle easily. True or False

3. When things don't go my way, I "lose it." True or False

4. I still get angry when I think of the bad things people did to me in the past. True or False

5. I find it very hard to forgive someone who has treated me badly. True or False

6. I often find myself engaged in heated arguments with the people who are close to me. True or False

7. At times I've felt angry enough to hurt someone. True or False

8. When riled, I often blurt out things which I later regret saying. True or False

9. When I get angry, frustrated or hurt, I comfort myself by eating or using alcohol or other drugs. True or False

10. I get angry with myself when I lose control of my emotions. True or False

11. When someone says or does something that upsets me, I don't usually say anything at the time, but later I spend a lot of time thinking of cutting replies I could and should have made. True or False

12. If I get really upset about something, I have a tendency to feel sick later (frequently experiencing weak spells, headaches, upset stomach or diarrhea). True or False

13. I am apt to take frustration so badly that I cannot put it out of my mind. True or False

14. I've been so angry at times I couldn't remember what I said or did. True or False

15. Sometimes I feel so hurt and alone that I've thought about hurting myself. True of False

16. Some people are afraid of my bad temper. True or False

17. I've become so angry at times that I've become physically violent, hitting other people or breaking things. True or False

18. When someone hurts me, I want to get even. True or False

19. People I've trusted have often let me down, leaving me feeling angry or betrayed. True or False

Scoring:

- If you answered **true for 10** or more questions – you might be prone to anger problems. You may need to consider seeking advice from a professional to help you deal with these anger issues.

- If you answered **true for 5** questions, your anger feelings are at an average level, however it might be beneficial learning some anger management and relaxation techniques.

Management Strategy:

1. Admit you have an anger problem.

2. Determine what you are going to do to help defeat the anger in your life.

3. Seek out professional help. Pastoral counseling, Christian counseling, anger management class.

4. Read all the passages in the Bible that address anger. Use a word search engine and look up the words anger and angry in the Bible.

5. Begin asking for prayer from those who are close to you by letting them know that you are trusting God for a new and graceful attitude.

Lesson 2- Understanding Anger

Often times anger will have us act out through aggression, rage, hostility, or violence. When we are angry it is easy to let our anger fuel our perception and behavior in response to a situation. It is difficult to learn how to control anger, but a promising first step is learning to understand our anger. Below are discussion questions to help you understand your anger.

What are the things that make you angry? Relationships, work, arguments, spouse, politics or something else.

How does your body feel when you get angry?

1. Tense

2. Heating up

3. Shaking

4. Tightening

5. Write out how you feel when angry:

____

____

____

____

How do you behave when you are angry?

1. Raising the volume of your voice

2. Cursing

3. Throw things

4. Hitting doors and walls

5. Hitting others

6. Saying nothing

7. Avoiding conflict

8. Walking away from the conflict

9. Write out how you behave when you are angry:

____

____

____

____

____

How does your angry behavior affect the situation?

1. People fear me

2. Nothing ever is resolved

3. Walls and doors need repair

4. I shut down and stop communication

5. I feel awful about my behavior

6. Write out how you think your angry behavior affect the situation:

____

____

____

What would you like to see change in regard to your anger?

1.   Keep my voice at a normal talking level

2.   Never use words that are insulting or foul

3.   Calm down before I speak

4.   Listen to the other person without thinking about my response

5.   Never throw things

6.   Never hit people or anything else

7.   Write out what you would like to see change in regard to your anger:

____

____

____

____

____

Describe the most recent situation when you felt angry. What happened? How did you behave? Did

the situation end with resolution?

1.   What happened?

____

____

____

____

____

2.   How did you behave?

---

3. Did the sitituation end with a resolution?

---

4. What have you discovered about anger and how anger looks on you?

Lesson 3 - What Do I Look Like When I Am Angry?

Draw a picture of what anger looks like.

Draw a picture in the box of what we want to do when we are angry.

How can we hurt others when we are angry? Finish the sentence. I tend to hurt those I am angry with by:

____

____

____

____

____

____

What should we do to calm down when we are angry?

(Circle the number that works for you).

1. Stop and practice slow breathing methods taking 10 to 15 slow and easy breaths. Inhaling and exhaling slow and easy.

2. Count to 20 taking in slow deep breaths and exhaling until you feel your heart rate slowing down.

3. Pause and pray. Heavenly Father, I am feeling very angry and I don't want to say or do the wrong thing. Please help me calm down so I can focus on how I should resolve the issue.

4. Tell the person that you are angry with that you need to stop the conversation and cool down before you discuss the problem.

5. Write out what has worked for you when you are trying to calm down and not lose your temper:

____

____

What should we do if we cannot control our anger?

1. Seek help from a counselor.

2. Attend an anger management class.

3. Ask for prayer from those who know and love you.

4. Admit you have a problem controlling your anger.

5. Seek help from your pastoral staff if you are a member of a church community.

6. Purchase a good anger management book and read it.

7. Write out your action plan:

____

____

____

____

____

____

____

____

____

____

____

Lesson 4 - Ten Types of Anger: What Is Yours?

Type 1: Assertive anger

Assertive anger is the most constructive type of anger expression. If this is your type of anger, you use feelings of frustration or rage as a catalyst for positive change. Rather than avoiding confrontation, internalizing anger, or resorting to verbal insults and physical outbursts, *you express your anger in ways that create change in the world around you – without causing distress or destruction.*

Management Strategy: (write your management strategy)

____

____

____

____

Type 2: Behavioral anger

Behavioral anger is expressed physically and is usually aggressive. If you've experienced this type of anger, you may feel so overwhelmed by your emotions that you lash out at the object of your rage. This might involve physically attacking someone or breaking or throwing things. This type of anger can be highly unpredictable and often has negative legal and interpersonal consequences.

Management Strategy: (write your management strategy)

____

____

____

Type 3: Chronic anger

Chronic anger is an ongoing, generalized resentment of other people, frustration with certain circumstances, and anger towards oneself. It's characterized by habitual irritation: the prolonged nature of this type of anger can have profoundly adverse effects on one's health and wellbeing.

Management Strategy: (write your management strategy)

____

____

____

____

____

Type 4: Judgmental anger

Judgmental anger is righteously indignant – this type of anger is usually a reaction to a perceived injustice or someone else's shortcoming. Although judgmental anger assumes a morally superior stance of justified fury, it may alienate potential allies by invalidating their difference of opinion.

Management Strategy: (write your management strategy)

____

____

____

____

____

Type 5: Overwhelmed anger

Overwhelmed anger is an uncontrolled type of anger. It usually occurs when we feel that a situation or circumstances are beyond our control, resulting in feelings of hopelessness and frustration. This type of anger is common when we've taken on too much responsibility, or unexpected life events have overthrown our usual capacity to cope with stress.

Management Strategy: (write your management strategy)

____

____

____

____

____

Type 6: Passive-aggressive anger

Passive-aggressive anger is an avoidant type of anger. If this is your usual mode of anger expression, you likely try to evade all forms of confrontation, and may deny or repress any feelings of frustration or fury you're experiencing. Passive-aggressive anger may be expressed verbally, as sarcasm, pointed silence or veiled mockery, or physically in behavior such as chronic procrastination at work. Sometimes people who express anger passively aren't even aware that their actions are perceived as aggressive – this can have dire personal and professional outcomes.

Management Strategy: (write your management strategy)

____

____

____

____

____

Type 7: Retaliatory anger

Retaliatory anger is usually an instinctual response to being confronted or attacked by someone else. It's one of the most common types of anger and is sometimes motivated by revenge for a perceived wrong. Retaliatory anger can also be deliberate and purposeful. It often aims to intimidate other people by asserting control over a situation or outcome yet may only serve to escalate tensions.

Management Strategy: (write your management strategy)

____

____

____

____

____

Type 8: Self-abusive anger

Self-abusive anger is a shame-based type of anger. If you've been feeling hopeless, unworthy, humiliated or ashamed, you might internalize those feelings and express anger via negative self-talk, self-harm, substance use, or eating disordered behavior. Alternatively, you may find yourself lashing out at those around to mask feelings of low self-worth, increasing your sense of alienation.

Management Strategy: (write your management strategy)

____

____

____

Type 9: Verbal anger

Verbal anger is often seen as less dangerous than behavioral anger, but it can be a form of emotional and psychological abuse that deeply hurts the target of one's anger. Verbal abuse may be expressed as furious shouting, threats, ridicule, sarcasm, intense blaming or criticism. If you've lashed out at someone verbally it's common to feel ashamed, apologetic and regretful afterwards.

Management Strategy: (write your management strategy)

____

____

____

____

____

Type 10: Volatile anger

Volatile anger seems to come out of nowhere: if this is your type of anger, you are very quick to get upset about perceived annoyances, both big and small. Once you've impulsively expressed your anger, you often calm down just as quickly. Unfortunately, volatile anger can be incredibly destructive, as those around you may feel they need to walk on eggshells for fear of triggering your rage. If left unchecked, volatile anger may eventually lead to violent outbursts.

Management Strategy: (write your management strategy)

____

____

____

Lesson 5- Identifying Anger Triggers: What makes you Angry?

Think back to the last few times you had an angry outburst and note:

What caused it?

____

____

____

____

What happened before it?

____

____

____

____

What were the events leading up to it?

____

____

____

____

What else happened that day?

Who were the people involved in the conflict?

How were you feeling before the conflict?

What triggers have you identified?

____

____

____

____

____

____

Lesson 6- Anger Warning Signs

Sometimes anger can affect what you say or do before you even recognize how you're feeling. You may become so used to the feeling of anger that you don't notice it, sort of like how you can hear the sound of an air condition, or the humming of a refrigerator, but block it from your mind.

Even if you aren't aware of your anger, it influences how you behave. The first step to managing anger is learning to recognize your personal warning signs that will tip you off about how you're feeling.

How do you react when you feel angry? Some of these warning signs might start when you are only a little irritated, and others might start when you are very angry.

Circle the warning signs that apply to you.

> Mind goes blank, Insult the other person, Face turns red, Body or hands shake Start sweating, Throw things, Heavy or fast breathing, Stare at the other person aggressively, Scowl or make an angry face, Scream, raise voice, or yell, Clench fists, Feel sick to the stomach, Punch walls, Feel hot, Become aggressive, Become argumentative, Go quiet and "shut down", Crying, Pace around the room, Headaches, Can't stop thinking about the problem.

Finish the sentence using the warning sign(s) that apply to you.

When I start getting angry I:

____

____

When I notice my warning signs, I will practice the following techniques that have proven to help me calm down and stay in control of me anger.

Calming Techniques

1. Take 10 to 20 slow breaths. Inhaling and exhaling slow and easy.

2. I will think about all the words I will speak. Using words that focus on the problem without insulting the person(s) that I am angry with.

3. I will be willing to walk away from conflict, waiting for another appointed time to discuss the matter.

4. I don't need to win the argument. I need to seek a resolution.

5. Admit that I am the problem.

6. I will seek forgiveness.

7. Always pray for each situation and all those who are involved.

Anger stop signs are clues that your body uses to let you know your anger is growing. These clues start to appear while your anger is still small. If you notice them in time, you can hit the brakes, and take control of your anger before it grows too big.

Everyone has their own anger stop sign. It's important to learn what yours are, so you can spot them in the future. Write your anger stop signs in the space below.

Common Anger Stop Signs

- My face feels hot

- I go quiet

- I can't think straight

- I start to shake

- My eyes get watery

- I feel annoyed.

- I raise my voice

- I try to bother people

- I want to hit something.

Lesson 7- When Anger Is A Problem

In small doses, anger is an appropriate, normal, and healthy emotion. Everyone experiences anger. It helps us stand up for ourselves when we've been wronged and hurt. However, in many circumstances, anger can have negative repercussions. Below are examples of how anger can be harmful and cause unwanted consequences.

Anger is a problem when it negatively affects others.

Anger drives people to act in a way that's unpleasant or harmful to those around them. This can result in straining or losing important relationships. It can be difficult to maintain healthy relationships when anger is out of control.

How much does this problem apply to you?

- Not at all

- Somewhat

- Very much

How has your anger impacted others?

____

____

____

____

____

____

Anger is a problem when it hinders performance at work or school.

Anger can lead to breakdowns in communication, making it difficult to work with others. Additionally, being preoccupied with anger harms one's ability to concentrate on work or school tasks.

How much does this problem apply to you?

- Not at all

- Somewhat

- Very much

How has anger negatively affected your performance at work or school?

____

____

____

____

____

____

Anger is a problem when it negatively affects health or well-being.

Anger affects both physical and emotional health. Physically, anger contributes to problems such as high blood pressure and heart attacks. Emotionally, anger contributes to anxiety, depression, and drug and alcohol use.

How much does this problem apply to you?

- Not at all

- Somewhat

- Very much

How has anger negatively affected your physical or emotional health?

____

____

____

____

Anger is a problem when it is too intense.

Even when anger is justified, it can be a problem if it goes too far. For example, physical aggression can lead to severe consequences such as physical harm to one's self or others, property damage, and legal trouble. A verbal outburst that's out of proportion to a situation may lead to losing a job, permanently damaging a relationship, or other consequences.

How much does this problem apply to you?

- Not at all

- Somewhat

- Very much

When was the last time your anger was too intense?

____

____

____

How are you planning on keeping your anger from becoming too intense?

____

____

____

Lesson 8- Anger Coping Skills

Six techniques for managing anger. Some of these skills can help to prevent or minimize explosive anger, such as triggers and warning signs. Other skills are intended to take control of anger, such as diversions, time-outs, and deep breathing.

Each skill has a brief description, and instructions on how it can be used. In session, make a point to practice each skill, and discuss when each one might be useful for your client. Additionally, stress the importance of practice, even when skills are not actively needed. Some anger coping skills, such as deep breathing, have long-last effects that can be helpful all day—not just in the heat of the moment.

Be Aware of Triggers

Anger triggers are the things that set you off. Knowing your triggers, and being cautious around them, will reduce the likelihood of your anger getting out of control.

How to use triggers to your advantage:

Create a list of your triggers and review them daily. Reviewing your triggers will keep them fresh in your mind; increasing the likelihood you notice them before they become a problem.

Oftentimes, the best way to deal with a trigger is to avoid it. This might mean making changes to your lifestyle, relationships, or daily routine.

Because it isn't always possible to avoid triggers, have a plan when you must face them. For example, avoid touchy conversations when you are tired, hungry, or upset.

Practice Deep Breathing

Deep breathing is a simple technique that's excellent for managing emotions. Not only is deep breathing effective, it's also discreet and easy to use at any time or place.

Sit comfortably and place one hand on your abdomen. Breathe in through your nose, deeply enough that the hand on your abdomen rises. Hold the air in your lungs, and then exhale slowly through your mouth, with your lips puckered as if you are blowing through a straw. The secret is to go slow: Time the inhalation (4s), pause (4s), and exhalation (6s). Practice for 3 to 5 minutes.

Keep an Anger Log

Following an episode of anger, take a few moments to record your experience. This practice will help you identify patterns, warning signs, and triggers, while also helping you organize thoughts and work through problems.

What was happening *before* the anger episode? Describe how you were feeling, and what was on your mind. Were you hungry, tired, or stressed?

Describe the facts of what happened. What events triggered your anger? How did you react, and did your reaction change as the event continued to unfold?

What were your thoughts and feelings *during* the anger episode? Looking back, do you see anything differently than when you were in the heat of the moment?[1]

---

[1] https://www.therapistaid.com/worksheets/coping-skills-anger.pdf

Use Diversions

The goal of diversions is to buy yourself time. If you can distract yourself for just 30 minutes, you'll have a better chance of dealing with your anger in a healthy way. Remember, you can always return to the source of your anger later—you're just setting the problem aside for now. Go for a walk watch a movie do yard work play a game play an instrument go hiking in nature.

Take a Time-out

Read a book practice a hobby draw or paint go for a bicycle ride call a friend take photographs play a sport go for a run do a craft write or journal lift weights play with a pet listen to music clean or organize cook or bake take a long bath go swimming rearrange a room.

Time-outs are a powerful tool for relationships where anger-fueled disagreements are causing problems. When someone calls a time-out, both individuals agree to walk away from the problem, and return once you have both had an opportunity to cool down.

How to use time-outs effectively:

With your partner, plan exactly how time-outs will work. Everyone should understand the rationale behind time-outs (an opportunity to cool down—not to avoid a problem).

What will you both do during time-outs? Plan activities that are in different rooms or different places. The list of diversions from above is a good place to begin.

Plan to return to the problem in 30 minutes to an hour. Important problems shouldn't be ignored forever, but nothing good will come from an explosive argument.

Know Your Warning Signs

Anger warning signs are the clues your body gives you that your anger is starting to grow. When you learn to spot your warning signs, you can begin to address your anger while it's still weak.

Sweating headaches pacing can't get past problem becoming argumentative aggressive body language feel hot / turn red raised voice feel sick to stomach clenched fists using verbal insults go quiet / "shut down".[2]

Lesson 9 - Anger Management Skills

Recognize your Anger Early

If you're yelling, it's probably too late. Learn the warning signs that you're getting angry so you can change the situation quickly. Some common signs are feeling hot, raising voices, balling of fists, shaking, and arguing.

Take a Timeout

Temporarily leave the situation that is making you angry. If other people are involved, explain to them that you need a few minutes alone to calm down. Problems usually aren't solved when one or more people are angry.

Deep Breathing

Take a minute to just breathe. Count your breaths: four seconds inhaling, four seconds holding your breath, and four seconds exhaling. Really keep track of time, or you might cheat yourself! The counting helps take your mind off the situation as well.

Exercise

Exercising serves as an emotional release. Chemicals released in your brain during the course of exercise create a sense of relaxation and happiness.

Express your Anger

Once you've calmed down, express your frustration. Try to be assertive, but not confrontational.

Expressing your anger will help avoid the same problems in the future.

Think of the Consequences

What will be the outcome of your next anger-fueled action? Will arguing convince the other person that you're right? Will you be happier after the fight?

Visualization

Imagine a relaxing experience. What do you see, smell, hear, feel, and taste? Maybe you're on a beach with sand between your toes and waves crashing in the distance. Spend a few minutes imagining every detail of your relaxing scene.

Lesson 10- Healthy Verses Unhealthy Coping Skills

Healthy vs. Unhealthy Coping Strategies

Coping strategies are actions we take--consciously or unconsciously--to deal with stress, problems, or uncomfortable emotions. Unhealthy coping strategies tend to feel good in the moment but have long-term negative consequences. Healthy coping strategies may not provide instant gratification, but they lead to long-lasting positive outcomes.

Examples of unhealthy coping strategies:

- Drug or alcohol use

- Overeating

- Procrastination

- Sleeping too much or too little

- Social withdrawal

- Self-harm

- Aggression

Examples of healthy coping strategies:

- Exercise

- Talking about your problem

- Healthy eating

- Seeking professional help

- Relaxation techniques (e.g. deep breathing)

- Using social support

- Problem-solving techniques

Example Scenarios

Noelle has a research paper due in one of her classes. Because the paper will require so much work, Noelle feels anxious every time she thinks about it. When Noelle distracts herself with other activities, she feels better. Noelle uses the coping strategy of procrastination to avoid her feelings of anxiety. This helps her feel better now but will cause problems in the long run.

- What consequences might result from Noelle's unhealthy coping strategy? (Answer below)

____

____

____

Juan feels jealous whenever his wife spends time with her friends. To control the situation, Juan uses insults to put down his wife's friends, and he demands that his wife stay home. When Juan's wife caves to his demands, he feels a sense of relief. Juan uses the coping strategy of aggression to avoid the discomfort of jealousy.

- What consequences might result from Juan's unhealthy coping strategy? (Answer below)

____

____

____

Rebecca is angry about being passed over for a promotion at work. Rather than discussing the situation with her boss and trying to improve her work performance, she holds onto her anger. Rebecca has learned to manage her anger by drinking alcohol. Drinking numbs Rebecca's anger temporarily, but the problems at work remain unresolved.

- What consequences might result from Rebecca's unhealthy coping strategy? (Answer below)

____

____

____

Lesson 11 – Anger Log

Anger has a way of sneaking up and taking control of our thoughts and actions before we realize what's happening. Fortunately, with practice, you can get better at catching your anger long before it takes over. Keeping an *Anger Diary* will help you achieve that goal.

Instructions: Either at the end of the day, or a few hours after your anger has passed, take a moment to reflect on a situation where you felt angry, or even just a bit frustrated. By following the example, take a few notes about the event. After recording five events, complete the review.

- What happened that made you angry?

  ____

  ____

  ____

- What provoked the situation?

  ____

  ____

  ____

- What did your body feel like as you were becoming more agitated?

  ____

  ____

  ____

- On a scale of 0-10 how angry did you feel?

  ____

- At what point did you stop listing to self-talk that was telling you to slow down and control your anger?

  ____

  ____

  ____

- What anger warning signs did you recognize?

  ____

- How many anger triggers did you ignore?

  ____

  ____

  ____

- At what point did you stop thinking about controlling anger?

  ____

  ____

  ____

- Were you more concerned about being angry or resolving to the conflict?

  ____

  ____

  ____

- What would you change about this incident?

  ____

  ____

  ____

After recording this information for a week or so, review your diary and look for reoccurring themes or "triggers" that make you angry. You'll also want to look for anger-triggering thoughts that reoccur again and again. One of the best and most successful methods for overcoming uncontrolled anger patterns is to become aware of how you are reacting and responding to those you are mad at. You will get better at self-awareness and self-control each time you review the anger log.

Lesson 12 - God's Answer for Anger

There are some people who make excuses for their anger. They say, "It just runs in my family." They are like a loaded shotgun with a hair trigger. Anytime they are jostled, they blast away. Then they say, "Oh, well, my anger only lasts a little while." Well, so do tornadoes, but look at what damage they can cause!

Let's see what the Bible, particularly the book of Proverbs has to say about being quick to get angry:

- "The discretion of a man deferreth his anger; and it is his glory to pass over a transgression. The king's wrath is as the roaring of a lion; but his favour is as dew upon the grass" (<u>Proverbs 19:11-12</u>).

- "A wrathful man stirreth up strife: but he that is slow to anger appeaseth strife" (<u>Proverbs 15:18</u>).

- "Go not forth hastily to strive, lest thou know not what to do in the end thereof, when thy neighbor hath put thee to shame" (<u>Proverbs 25:8</u>).

When you are quick to get angry, you can lose so much — your job, friends, children, wife, health, testimony — there is nothing more debilitating to your Christian testimony than to be known as one who is quick to anger.

What should we do with our anger?

Step 1 - Confess Anger

If we repress our anger rather than confess it, our anger can do all kinds of damage. You may say that you're not angry, but your stomach will keep the score. So, the first thing you must do to control your anger is to confess it to the Lord. Tell Him, "There's something moving in me I don't like. And I need the Holy Spirit to take control of me and prevent me from acting uncontrollably or unholy."

Someone has well said that if you repress anger it is like lighting a wastebasket, putting it in a closet, and closing the door. It may burn itself out or it may burn the house down. If you want to get control, the very first thing you need to do is open the closet door and say. "There it is, Lord. It's in there. Put out the fire."

Step 2 - Consider Anger

When you take a step back from your anger and begin to seek understanding from the Lord, He will show you the answer. It is so important to analyze the source of your anger, so you don't go off half-cocked. <u>Psalm 4:4</u> says, "Stand in awe, and sin not: commune with your own heart upon your bed and be still."

God promises He will show us the way if we will seek Him. "I will instruct thee and teach thee in the way which thou shalt go: I will guide thee with Mine eye" (<u>Psalm 32:8</u>). And don't look around at the world to see how they are handling it, look to God. <u>Romans 12:2</u> says, "And be not conformed to this world: but be ye transformed by the renewing of your mind, that ye may prove what is that good, and acceptable, and perfect, will of God."

Step 3 - Control Anger

Now, you're ready to work on controlling your anger. You say, "I can't control it." Oh, yes you can. One day you may be having one of those discussions that can be heard about two blocks away and suddenly your cell phone rings. You stop the loud talk and softly say, "Hello." Now, don't tell me you can't turn anger on and off. You can! <u>Proverbs 29:11</u> says, "A fool uttereth all his mind: but a wise man keepeth it in till afterwards." Fools spout off anything and everything, but a wise man can choose to control his tongue.

There it is, confess, consider, and control. Now, I don't guarantee that you will no longer struggle with anger, but if you can get down these basics, you are well on your way. [3]

Obey the Scripture

"But be ye doers of the word, and not hearers only, deceiving your own selves." (James 1:22 KJV)

Most of the time anger is a sin, but not all the time. Righteous anger or biblical anger is not sinful. When we are angry about the sin going on in the world or angry at the way others are being treated, that is an example of biblical anger.

Biblical anger is concerned about others and it usually results in a solution to problems. Anger is sinful when it comes from an impatient, prideful, unforgiving, untrusting, and wicked heart.

Quick Bible References for Anger

But be ye doers of the word, and not hearers only, deceiving your own selves. (James 1:22 KJV)

1. Psalms 37:8-9 - Cease from anger and forsake wrath: fret not thyself in any wise to do evil.

2. Proverbs 12:16 - A fool's wrath is presently known: but a prudent [man] covereth shame.

3. Proverbs 14:17 - [He that is] soon angry dealeth foolishly: and a man of wicked devices is hated.

4. Proverbs 15:1 - A soft answer turneth away wrath: but grievous words stir up anger.

5. Proverbs 15:18 - A wrathful man stirreth up strife: but [he that is] slow to anger appeaseth strife.

6. Proverbs 16:32 - [He that is] slow to anger [is] better than the mighty; and he that ruleth his spirit than he that taketh a city.

7. Proverbs 19:11 - The discretion of a man deferreth his anger; and [it is] his glory to pass over a transgression.

8. Proverbs 22:24 - Make no friendship with an angry man; and with a furious man thou shalt not go:

9. Proverbs 29:11 - A fool uttereth all his mind: but a wise [man] keepeth it in till afterwards.

10. Ecclesiastes 7:9 - Be not hasty in thy spirit to be angry: for anger resteth in the bosom of fools.

11. Matthew 5:22 - But I say unto you, That whosoever is angry with his brother without a cause shall be in danger of the judgment: and whosoever shall say to his brother, Raca, shall be in danger of the council: but whosoever shall say, Thou fool, shall be in danger of hell fire.

12. Luke 6:31 - And as ye would that men should do to you, do ye also to them likewise.

13. Romans 12:21 - Be not overcome of evil, but overcome evil with good.

14. Ephesians 4:26-27 - Be ye angry, and sin not: let not the sun go down upon your wrath:

15. Ephesians 4:26 - Be ye angry, and sin not: let not the sun go down upon your wrath:

16. Ephesians 4:31 - Let all bitterness, and wrath, and anger, and clamour, and evil speaking, be put away from you, with all malice:

17. Colossians 3:8 - But now ye also put off all these; anger, wrath, malice, blasphemy, filthy communication out of your mouth.

18. James 1:19-20 - Wherefore, my beloved brethren, let every man be swift to hear, slow to speak, slow to wrath:

19. James 1:19 - Wherefore, my beloved brethren, let every man be swift to hear, slow to speak, slow to wrath:

20. James 1:20 - For the wrath of man worketh not the righteousness of God.

21. James 4:1-2 - From whence [come] wars and fightings among you? [come they] not hence, [even] of your lusts that war in your members?

Quotes and Saying About Anger

1. "The best fighter is never angry." — Lao Tzu

2. "Speak when you are angry and you will make the best speech you will ever regret." — Ambrose Bierce

3. "Holding on to anger is like grasping a hot coal with the intent of throwing it at someone else; you are the one who gets burned." — Buddha

4. "Never respond to an angry person with a fiery comeback, even if he deserves it...Don't allow his anger to become your anger."

   — Bohdi Sanders, Warrior Wisdom: Ageless Wisdom for the Modern Warrior

5. "The greatest remedy for anger is delay." — Thomas Paine

6. "Angry people want you to see how powerful they are... loving people want you to see how powerful You are." — Chief Red Eagle

7. "The first key to leadership was self-control, particularly the mastery of pride, which was something more difficult, he explained, to subdue than a wild lion and anger, which was more difficult to defeat than the greatest wrestler. He warned them that "if you can't swallow your pride, you can't lead." — Jack Weatherford, Genghis Khan and the Making of the Modern World

8. "Do not let your anger lead to hatred, as you will hurt yourself more than you would the other." — Stephen Richards

9. "Fear is based on ignorance. Lack of understanding is also a primary cause of anger." — Thich Nhat Hanh, Reconciliation: Healing the Inner Child

10. "Get mad and get over it." - Colin Powell

11. "Men are like steel. When they lose their temper, they lose their worth." – Chuck Norris

12. "Men is rage strike those who mean them best." – William Shakespeare

13. "Being anger is human. Staying angry is foolish." T.D. Jakes

14. "It is wise to direct your anger towards problems - not people; to focus your energies on answers - not excuses." – William Arthur Ward

15. "Anger is an acid that can do more harm to the vessel in which it is stored than to anything on which it is poured." – Mark Twain

16. "People who fly into rage always make a bad landing." – Will Rogers

17. "One who is slow to anger is better than the mighty; one who rules his spirit, than he who takes a city." – Solomon

18. "Anger and folly walk cheek and jowl." – Ben Franklin

19. "For every minute you remain angry, you give up sixty seconds of peace of mind." – Ralph Waldo Emerson

20. "I would rather just be kindhearted than angry spirited." – Skip Pilgrim

Bible Study for Overcoming Anger

As God's children, we can all make this journey of change together. Here are some things I have learned over the years in my fight against sinful anger. Understanding and applying these truths to your own life will help you overcome sinful anger and see sustained fruit.

1. Anger has three faces: It is expressed primarily in three different ways:

1) Explosive and blowing up.

2) Stewing, brewing, or silent indignation.

3) Irritability, exasperation or embitterment.

Silent anger is just as offensive to God as explosive anger. How are you prone to express your anger? (Write out your answer)

____

____

____

____

2. Anger hurts relationships: You choose who is on the receiving end of your anger because anger is a perceived threat to something you hold valuable. The problem is we can go a whole day at work being "nice" to our co-workers only to lose it at home with those closest to us! We tend to take it out on those we are called to love the most. Who has been on the receiving end of your anger the most? (Write out your answer)

____

____

____

____

3. Anger is in the Bible: The Bible has a lot to say about anger. From the beginning in the garden all the way to the end; man's anger is expressed by rejecting God and pursuing his own way (Romans 3:10–18). Yet man's anger does not accomplish God's righteous purposes (James 1:19–20). While God too can be angry, it is never sinful (Psalm 7:11; John 3:36; Romans 1:18). Actually, compared to the offenses He must suffer, He is very "slow to anger" (Exodus 34:6; Psalm 103:8). Does your anger accomplish God's purposes? (Write out your answer)

____

____

____

4. Anger put Jesus on the cross: Did you know that the anger of man and God's wrath for all our sins culminated onto Jesus when he went to the cross to pay the penalty for sin (Acts 2:22–24)? He satisfied God's wrath and allowed man to express their anger towards him at the same time—man rejecting God and God loving man in the very same event in history. How often do you reject God in your anger by not doing what He calls you to do? (Write out your answer)

5. Anger is covered by Christ's blood: The blood of Christ is sufficient to cover your sinful anger. No matter what wrath has protruded from your mouth or what you've done physically to harm others or yourself, you can be forgiven and walk in newness of life. Anger is a sin, but the death of Christ is payment enough to cover it. If you have died with Christ, you can become a different person (Romans 6:5–11).

Do you believe and live as if your anger is covered by the blood of Christ or do you act like

His blood isn't sufficient? Why or why not? (Write out your answer)

____

____

____

____

6. Anger is a life-dominating sin: Just like any other "addiction," we become enslaved to anger. It temporarily satisfies our sinful desire and flesh, yet we feel guilty and ashamed when we give full vent to it. It's a vicious cycle of self-destruction. Are you stuck in a vicious cycle of anger? If so, you can be set free (1 Corinthians 6:9–11). (Write out your answer)

____

____

____

____

7. Anger is an expression of false worship: Like all other "addictions," anger has false worship at its core. When you express your anger sinfully, ask yourself, "What am I not getting that I really want or that I'm willing to sin to get?" Your answer will reveal what you're living for in that moment. Something else has captured your heart more than God, and you're seeking a false refuge; that is idolatry. What's captured your heart more than God? (Write out your answer)

____

____

____

____

8. Anger is often just a fruit: It usually has fear at the root and more specifically, it is the fear of man. While anger may be all we can see at times, at the heart of it is a fearful, insecure, unsafe, untrusting heart looking for something from man that only God can satisfy. Learn to love God more with reverent awe and fear because then you'll learn to need people less. Remember that perfect love casts out fear (1 John 4:18) and that you are perfectly loved by your heavenly Father. What are you really afraid of deep down in the innermost being of your heart? (Write out your answer)

____

____

____

____

9. Anger can be righteous: Ephesians 4:26 says, "Be angry and do not sin." You express righteous anger by becoming angry about what angers God. Jesus died not only to free you from sinful anger but to enable you to be angry with God not at God. Is your anger expressed righteously or sinfully? How can you tell? Would others say the same?

10. Anger must be surrendered: The only way out is to surrender your anger to God. Do not control or manage it in your flesh. Let the Spirit move you to action or bring you to brokenness. God is the judge, not you or me (James 4:11–12). Are you ready to step down from the throne of your mini judgment seat and allow God to be God? Remember, "vengeance is mine," says the Lord (Romans 12:18–21).

Are you ready to humble yourself in your broken state and surrender your sinful anger to God? Know that He will give you grace in your time of need (Isaiah 66:2b; 2 Chronicles 16:9; James 4:6). So, if you are ready, repent, ask God and those you have offended to forgive you, and walk in victory over the sinful anger that's held you captive for so long. (Answer yes or no) ____________.

A Final Thought About Anger

My childhood memories are of my mother and father fighting and arguing over everything under the sun. The fights were brutal that included some of the most horrible name calling matches one could ever attend. I have seen my mother weeping and wanting to take me and leave the battle torn field of our home, and often wished that she would have done just that. I grew up in a dysfunctional, and domestic abusive home that caused me to have anger issues through-out my adult life.

God's Word is truth, and because of the Bible, and my faith in Jesus Christ I have been able to forgive my parents for giving me a hard and difficult childhood. Both mom and dad have passed from this earth into eternity to be with the Lord, and I remain on my earthly mission to help those who are dealing with anger, depression, anxiety, addictions and post -traumatic stress disorders.

My thoughts are resting in the following words written by Dorothy Law Nolte.

- If children live with criticism, they learn to condemn.

- If children live with hostility, they learn to fight.

- If children live with fear, they learn to be apprehensive.

- If children live with pity, they learn to feel sorry for themselves.

- If children live with ridicule, they learn to feel shy.

- If children live with jealousy, they learn to feel envy.

- If children live with shame, they learn to feel guilty.

- If children live with encouragement, they learn confidence.

- If children live with tolerance, they learn patience.

- If children live with praise, they learn appreciation.

- If children live with acceptance, they learn to love.

- If children live with approval, they learn to like themselves.

- If children live with recognition, they learn it is good to have a goal.

- If children live with sharing, they learn generosity.

- If children live with honesty, they learn truthfulness.

- If children live with fairness, they learn justice.

- If children live with kindness and consideration, they learn respect.

- If children live with security, they learn to have faith in themselves and in those about them.

- If children live with friendliness, they learn the world is a nice place in which to live.[4]

Other works authored by Dr. Pilgrim:

- 101 Stress Tips
- 12 Steps To Freedom From Stress (Workbook)
- 12 Steps To Freedom From Addictions (Workbook)
- Understanding And Controlling Anger

www.ingramcontent.com/pod-product-compliance
Lightning Source LLC
Chambersburg PA
CBHW081632250726
48657CB00009B/2849